ADRENALIN!

Surfing

Paul Mason

Chrysalis Children's Books

First published in the UK in 2005 by
Chrysalis Children's Books
An imprint of the Chrysalis Books Group Plc
The Chrysalis Building, Bramley Road,
London W10 6SP

ISBN 1 84458 399 6

British Library Cataloguing in Publication Data for this book is available
from the British Library.

Associate Publisher Joyce Bentley
Senior editor Rasha Elsaeed
Project editors Jon Richards and Kate Simkins
Editorial assistant Camilla Lloyd
Designer Ed Simkins
Picture researcher Lorna Ainger
Consultant Mike Searle
Mike founded *ThreeSixty* bodyboard magazine in 1991. Since then he has worked as
senior photographic contributor to *Carve* surfing magazine.

Produced by Tall Tree Ltd, UK

Printed in China

10 9 8 7 6 5 4 3 2 1

Typography Natascha Frensch
Read Regular, READ SMALLCAPS and Read Space; European Community Design Registration 2003
and Copyright © Natascha Frensch 2001-2004 Read Medium, **Read Black** and *Read Slanted*
Copyright © Natascha Frensch 2003-2004

READ™ is a revolutionary new typeface that will enhance children's understanding through clear,
easily recognisable character shapes. With its evenly spaced and carefully designed characters,
READ™ will help children at all stages to improve their literacy skills, and is ideal for young readers,
reluctant readers and especially children with dyslexia.

Disclaimer
In preparation of this book all due care has been exercised with regard to the advice, activities
and techniques depicted. The publishers regret that they can accept no liability for any loss or
injury sustained. When learning a new sport it is important to get expert tuition and to follow
any manufacturers' instructions.

Picture acknowledgments
All reasonable efforts have been made to ensure the reproduction of content has been done with
the consent of copyright owners. If you are aware of any unintentional omissions please contact
the publishers directly so that any necessary corrections may be made for future editions.
Bishop Museum: 6, 26, Pete Frieden: 17br, Leroy Grannis: 8, Tim McKenna: 28
Chris Power: 4-5, 9, 10–11, 12–13, 15tr, 19b, 25r
Mike Searle: cover, 1, 3, 14, 16, 18–19, 20–21, 22–23, 25l, 27r, 32
Tostee/ASP: 29, Alex Williams: 13, 15c, 17tl, 24, 27l, Doug Wilson: 7

Contents

Catching the wave

Surfing is the art of riding waves. Since its development within the waters around the islands of the Pacific, surfing has spread across the world, influencing many aspects of culture, including fashion, films and music.

Catching waves

Surfing has been described as 'walking on water' and brings people as close as possible to the raw and awesome power of nature. Small wonder then that it is incredibly popular, and thousands of people are out on the water every day, catching waves all around the world, from exotic, tropical resorts to the seas off chilly, windswept beaches.

THE BEST SURFERS MAKE CATCHING A WAVE LOOK EASY. HOWEVER, THEY HAVE HAD TO PRACTISE FOR MANY HOURS TO BE THIS GOOD.

Styles of surfing

There are several different styles of surfing today. Many surfers ride shortboards. Others ride longboards, which are just under 3m long. A few surfers use kneeboards, which they kneel on after catching the wave. One of the most popular types of surfing is bodyboarding where people lie on a very short board to ride waves.

SURFERS WATCH THE WAVES POUNDING THE SHORE AT SEIGNOSSE ON THE FRENCH ATLANTIC COAST.

The language of surfing

Here are a few surf words that might help you bluff your way through a conversation with a surfer.

GROMMET A young surfer.

HO-DAD A non-surfer or uncool person.

KAHUNA Hawaiian royalty; an older surfer worthy of respect.

KOOK A bad or inexperienced surfer.

WAHINE Hawaiian for a girl or woman.

The roots of surfing

The first surfers were Polynesian people who populated the thousands of islands in the Pacific Ocean. Polynesians have surfed since around 2000 BC, but it was the Hawaiians who first stood up on their boards.

The sport of wave riding

The islands of Hawaii are in the middle of the Pacific Ocean. Waves roll into the islands' shores continuously, and surfing has been an important part of Hawaiian culture for hundreds of years. The Hawaiian chiefs rode giant *olo* boards. These were so heavy that it took several people to carry them. Only these *olo* boards could catch the biggest waves. Ordinary Hawaiians rode *alaia* boards, which were shorter and less heavy.

THIS ETCHING DATING FROM 1851 SHOWS HAWAIIANS TAKING PART IN THE 'SPORT OF SURF PLAYING'.

SURFING REALLY STARTED TO TAKE OFF IN THE 1950S, HELPED BY THE DEVELOPMENT OF NEW TECHNOLOGY. THESE SURFERS FROM THE 1960S ARE HOLDING LONGBOARDS MADE FROM ARTIFICIAL MATERIALS.

Across the Pacific

Surfing spread to the USA in 1907. George Freeth came from Hawaii to demonstrate surfing at Huntington Beach, Los Angeles. A local surf scene soon sprang up in California. Around the same time, tourists at Waikiki Beach in Hawaii began to take surfing lessons. In 1914, Hawaii's champion swimmer, Duke Kahanamoku, visited Australia where he gave surfing demonstrations. Riding a board he had made himself, he rode the waves at Freshwater Beach, Sydney, for three hours. Duke also visited towns on the US East Coast, such as Atlantic City. The surfing demonstrations given by George Freeth and Duke Kahanamoku helped to spread surfing around the world.

Surfing conquers the world

By the beginning of the 1960s, surfing had started to feature in films. Towards the end of the 20th century, it had become part of mainstream fashion with many people copying the 'surfer look' of baggy shorts and surf T-shirts.

Surfing on screen

In 1959, a film called *Gidget* came out. It told the story of a young Californian girl who was determined to learn to surf. The publicity posters for *Gidget* asked, 'Who's got time for Adults?'. At the same time, surf music became popular – bands like The Beach Boys were blaring out of every teenager's radio. Suddenly, everyone wanted to surf.

MIKEY DORA WAS A SURFING LEGEND THROUGHOUT THE 1950S AND 1960S. HE APPEARED IN A NUMBER OF MOVIES FROM THE PERIOD, INCLUDING *Gidget*, *Beach Party* (1963) AND *Ride the Wild Surf* (1964).

SURF FACT

Two inventions revolutionised surfing in 1971. The leash meant that surfers no longer had to swim to collect their boards, and the boogie board made surfing far easier for beginners.

'Locals only!'

Other surfing films followed on after the success of *Gidget*, including *The Endless Summer* (1964). They went a long way to making surfing even more popular. However, surfing's increased popularity also meant that waves got very crowded. Local surfers tried to stop 'outsiders' by painting 'Locals Only!' slogans near beaches.

A Film by BRUCE BROWN

The Endless Summer

The original 1964 surfing classic

The Endless Summer FOLLOWED A GROUP OF SURFERS AROUND THE WORLD IN THEIR SEARCH FOR THE PERFECT WAVE.

SURFERS TODAY BENEFIT FROM MODERN TECHNOLOGY. WOODEN BOARDS HAVE BEEN REPLACED BY ONES MADE FROM FIBREGLASS AND FOAM, MAKING THEM LIGHTER AND STRONGER.

The big time

More and more people took up surfing throughout the 1970s and 1980s. The sport really hit the big time in the 1990s, when outdoor sports of all kinds became popular. Surfing, with its healthy, beach-based lifestyle, proved especially attractive. The sport also appeared in adverts for everything from drinks to cars. Films such as *Point Break* (1991) and *In God's Hands* (1998) took surfing to inland audiences and 'surf shops' far from the ocean also began selling surf clothing.

Surfing equipment

Surfers all have their own idea of what makes a great surfboard. They know that decisions about the length, width, thickness and shape will affect how the board rides when they finally take it out in the surf.

Long or short?

Surfers use different boards for different types of waves or for the style of ride they want. For example, longboards can be great for having a slow, relaxing surf, while twin-fins can be excellent if you are feeling energetic. Longboards are usually about 2.75 m long and 0.6 m wide. They are easy to learn on because they are more stable than shortboards. Guns are long, narrow boards for riding big surf. Tow-in boards have footstraps and lead weights inside to make them easier to control on giant waves.

The bottom shape of most boards is either flat, vee or concave.

The tail shape can be squash-tail, swallowtail, pin-tail or rounded-pin.

Surfing accessories

WAX	Rubbed on the deck of the board to help the surfer's feet grip.
DECK GRIP	Stuck on the board for extra grip. Tail patches are the most popular type of deck grip.
LEASHES	Keep the board and surfer attached to one another when the surfer falls off (also called leg ropes or kook cords).
BOARD BAGS	For storing the board in – can be padded for extra protection.

The amount of curve of a board when seen from the side is called its 'rocker'.

This board has a narrow nose for lighter weight and increased manoeuvrability.

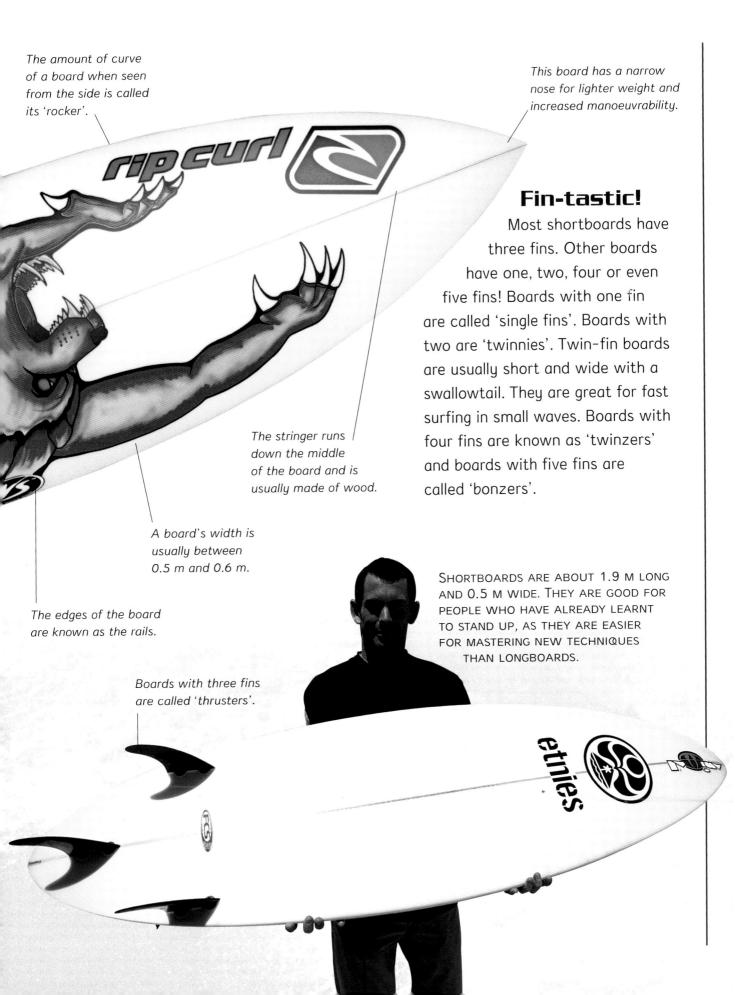

Fin-tastic!

Most shortboards have three fins. Other boards have one, two, four or even five fins! Boards with one fin are called 'single fins'. Boards with two are 'twinnies'. Twin-fin boards are usually short and wide with a swallowtail. They are great for fast surfing in small waves. Boards with four fins are known as 'twinzers' and boards with five fins are called 'bonzers'.

The stringer runs down the middle of the board and is usually made of wood.

A board's width is usually between 0.5 m and 0.6 m.

The edges of the board are known as the rails.

SHORTBOARDS ARE ABOUT 1.9 M LONG AND 0.5 M WIDE. THEY ARE GOOD FOR PEOPLE WHO HAVE ALREADY LEARNT TO STAND UP, AS THEY ARE EASIER FOR MASTERING NEW TECHNIQUES THAN LONGBOARDS.

Boards with three fins are called 'thrusters'.

Surf clothing

In the water, surfers wear the minimum needed to keep warm. In Queensland, California or Bali, this may be a pair of shorts, while in Cornwall, Norway or Maine, cold seas make a wetsuit essential.

Loose and baggy

Over the years, surfers have developed their own style of clothing. Out of the water they tend to wear loose-fitting clothes that are easy to get on and off when getting changed for a surf session. Lots of layers help to keep surfers warm after surfing in a cold sea. Hooded tops, loose T-shirts and baggy shorts are all part of the surfer style.

SURF WEAR IS NOW PART OF EVERYDAY FASHION, WITH HIGH-STREET SHOPS SELLING HOODED TOPS AND SURF T-SHIRTS.

GETTING READY FOR A SURF SESSION USUALLY MEANS A QUICK CHANGE NEXT TO THE SURFERS' CAR OR VAN.

WETSUITS WORK BY TRAPPING A LAYER OF WATER BETWEEN THE SKIN AND THE SUIT. THIS REDUCES THE RATE AT WHICH HEAT IS LOST FROM THE BODY.

A wetsuit needs to be tight-fitting to trap water against the body.

When it's warm

In warm water, surfers wear as little as possible. Usually for men, this is just a pair of shorts. These are about knee-length so that the hems do not rub as the surfer sits on the board. Board shorts often have a pocket for keys, wax or money to be kept in. Some surfers also wear what is called a 'rash vest' to keep off the sun's harmful rays.

When it's cold

The main aim in cool water is to keep warm, and the key piece of clothing for this is a wetsuit. Some wetsuits cover about as much of a surfer's body as a T-shirt and shorts. These are known as 'shorties' and are used in warmer water. In colder water, surfers wear suits that leave only their hands, feet and head uncovered. When it is really cold, surfers wear gloves, boots and a hood, too.

Building a board

Years ago, surfers made their own boards out of wood. Today, surfboards are made in a variety of high-tech ways using computer technology and the latest artificial materials.

The blank

Most surfboards today are made of polystyrene foam and fibreglass. The board is shaped from a foam 'blank'. This is a surfboard-shaped piece of foam with a wooden strip, called a 'stringer', running up the middle. The stringer gives the finished board strength. Shaping is a very delicate business, and the majority of shapers make their measurements in millimetres.

THESE SURFBOARD BLANKS ARE READY FOR SHAPING. YOU CAN CLEARLY SEE THE WOODEN STRINGERS THAT RUN DOWN THE MIDDLE OF EACH BOARD.

Shaping

The shape of the board is all important to its performance. Today, some surfboard factories have shaping computers. These are programmed to control a shaping machine. They can create exact copies of successful surfboards.

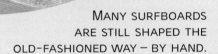

MANY SURFBOARDS ARE STILL SHAPED THE OLD-FASHIONED WAY – BY HAND.

SHAPING AND GLASSING IS MESSY WORK AND BOARD MAKERS NEED TO WEAR MASKS TO PROTECT THEIR LUNGS FROM THE POTENTIALLY HARMFUL DUST.

Glassing

Once the maker is happy with the shape of the board, it is 'glassed'. This means it is coated with layers of fibreglass to give it strength and stiffness. Usually, two layers of fibreglass are added to the deck and one to the bottom. Once the fibreglass has dried, the board is ready to use.

SURF FACT

In Australia, money is waterproof, allowing surfers to carry their notes into the surf.

What makes the surf?

As well as the shape and style of the board, the shape and style of the waves as they crash on the shore can have an enormous impact on the type of ride that a surfer experiences.

The crest is the part of the wave that has just broken or is about to break.

The pocket is the part of the wave just in front of the whitewater.

The whitewater is the part of the wave that has already broken.

The face is the front part of the wave in front of the breaking crest.

Ocean ripples

The waves surfers like best come from 'groundswell'. This is created by high winds out at sea. The winds blow over the ocean creating ripples. When these ripples reach a coast, the shallow bottom lifts them up to become waves. When groundswell hits a gently sloping beach, the waves break slowly. Groundswell hitting a steeply sloping beach or a reef will create tall waves with steep faces.

MANY EXPERIENCED SURFERS PREFER THE THRILL OF RIDING TALL WAVES. BUT SOME ARE TOO BIG, EVEN FOR THE BEST SURFER.

Surf styles

The type of shore that a wave breaks against can create different styles of surf. 'Beach breaks' have sandy or pebbly bottoms. 'Reef-break' waves usually break in the same place and in the same way, making it easier to know where to catch the waves. 'Point-break' waves appear where groundswell hits land that sticks out to sea. Sandbanks in river mouths create 'rivermouth breaks' that are a cross between a point break and a beach break.

CATCHING A TUBE IS ONE OF THE BIGGEST THRILLS IN SURFING.

Catching the tube

Sometimes groundswell reaches shallow water suddenly. This causes the water at the top of the wave to pitch forwards quickly, creating a very steep wave face. Occasionally, a cylinder is formed by the wave – surfers call this the 'tube'.

Different surf breaks

Here are a few famous places with different types of surf break:

POINT BREAK Malibu, California   **REEF BREAK** G-land, Indonesia
RIVERMOUTH BREAK Mundaka, Spain   **BEACH BREAK** Supertubes, Portugal

Surfing start-up

At first, trying to stand on a surfboard feels a bit like trying to stand up on a galloping horse. Then, suddenly, you manage to get to your feet and ride in to the beach, wearing a wetsuit and a big smile.

Surf school

The best place to learn to surf is at a beach that has lifeguards. Lots of people learn by taking classes, where you get to use the surf school's wetsuits and boards. Others learn to surf with their friends giving them some lessons and the loan of some equipment.

The takeoff

The first aim of surfing is to catch the wave and stand up, called the 'takeoff'.

1. As the wave arrives, paddle quickly to get the board travelling with the wave.

2. Once moving with the wave, the aim is to stand up in one movement, firstly by placing your hands on the board.

3. With your weight on your hands, bring your feet forwards quickly and smoothly and position them across the centre line of the board.

4. Now try to stand on the board, making sure that you keep your balance as the board travels with the wave.

Steering

Once you have mastered standing on the board, try steering it along the wave. To turn, surfers put a little more weight on their back foot. This lifts the nose and allows the board to pivot round. Having turned along the wave, surfers use foot pressure to make the board rise and fall on the wave. More weight on the back foot makes the board rise up the face of the wave. More weight on the front foot pushes it down the face. These movements are called 'trimming' the board.

Reaching the waves

When paddling a surfboard, surfers try to keep the nose of the board just out of the water. If it is sticking up too far, you will be pushing the board through the water instead of gliding on top of it.

MANY SURFERS PRACTISE THE TAKEOFF ON DRY LAND BEFORE PADDLING OUT TO TRY IT ON FLAT WATER.

Advanced surfing

Once surfers have learnt the basics of taking off and trimming, they are ready to learn more advanced techniques. These are the spectacular moves that allow them to race up and down a wave and glide along it.

Cutback

This technique is used to get back to the 'pocket', the part of the wave just in front of the breaking crest. In a cutback, the surfer makes a quick, hard turn out on the face of the wave, so that the board is heading back towards the pocket. Then the surfer turns again, this time to point away from the pocket.

A SURFER PERFORMING A CUTBACK AT THE TOP OF THE WAVE.

Top turn

The uppermost part of a wave, where it is just about to break, is the most powerful part. Doing a turn here allows surfers to pick up more speed as they drop back down the face of the wave. Top turns are made by putting the weight on the back foot to lever the board around.

LEAVE IT TOO LATE TO PULL A TOP TURN AND YOU COULD END UP FLYING OFF THE TOP OF THE WAVE!

Bottom turn

This is the most important advanced technique. After catching a wave, the board picks up speed as it races down the face. At the bottom of the face, the surfer uses a bottom turn to turn sideways and back up the face of the wave. Surfers bend at the waist and knees and put extra weight on their back foot. They use their toes or heels to lean the board around.

TIMING IS CRITICAL ON A BOTTOM TURN. TURN TOO LATE AND YOU LOSE ALL YOUR SPEED AND GET SWALLOWED BY THE WAVE. TURN TOO SOON AND THE FINS MAY SLIP, CAUSING YOU TO FALL OFF.

Surf safety

The ocean is a dangerous place and surfers are killed every year – even the most experienced surfer can get into trouble. Crowded waves also create hazards, especially when surfers do not obey the rules.

On your own

The most important rule for staying alive in the ocean is to be 100 per cent certain that you will be able to get back to shore. Once you are out in the surf, lifeguards or other surfers may be able to help you – but they may not. Surfers know that they are responsible for their own safety and should not rely on anyone else.

SPECIALLY TRAINED LIFEGUARDS PATROL MANY BEACHES AND HELP SURFERS WHO GET INTO TROUBLE.

Crowds

Each year, more and more people take up surfing. As the surf spots become more crowded, the chances of being hit by someone else's board are more likely. To prevent this, surfers follow the rules of surfing.

DROPPING IN ON ANOTHER PERSON'S WAVE IS ONE OF THE WORST THINGS A SURFER CAN DO.

Ocean hazards

One of the biggest dangers is rip currents (also called undertow). These happen when all the water pushed onto the beach by big waves has to get back to sea. It flows out at the deepest part of the beach and can easily drag unwary people out to sea or under the surface. Another danger for surfers is shallow bottoms. Several famous surfers have been killed after hitting their heads on the bottom, and some people wear special helmets to avoid this.

Basic surf rules

1 The surfer closest to the peak has the right to ride the wave.
2 If a wave has several peaks, the first surfer to his or her feet has the right to ride the wave.
3 Breaking rules 1 and 2 is called 'dropping in'. Never drop in on another surfer.
4 A surfer riding a wave is responsible for avoiding swimmers and paddling surfers. They do not have to get out of the rider's way.
5 Hold on to your board while paddling out. If you let go, it could hit someone.

Improving in the surf

There are surfers of all levels and abilities. Some are happy to catch smaller waves and glide along them. Others want to ride big surf or enter competitions. Some even dream of being world champion one day.

Muscle power

All surfers need endurance. This allows them to keep paddling for hours. There are lots of ways to train for endurance. Going for a long paddle on your board on a flat day is one way to increase endurance. Swimming is also good, as are running and cycling. Surfers also need power in order to sprint quickly to catch a wave. Most rely on their endurance training to give them power as well.

SURF FACT

In competitions, qualifying heats usually last for 30 minutes. The surfers are constantly paddling through the surf and need to be very fit to do this.

BEACH RUNNING IS GOOD ENDURANCE TRAINING AS SAND IS A VERY TIRING SURFACE TO RUN ON.

Flexible

Flexibility helps surfers to twist their bodies and allows them to perform the hardest surfing techniques. Balance also helps with this. Yoga is becoming increasingly popular as a way of developing both flexibility and balance.

STRETCHING THE LEGS AND BACK BEFORE SURFING HELPS MUSCLES PERFORM AT THEIR PEAK FROM THE START.

Top-level surfing

Some surfers aim to become good enough to enter competitions. They usually start with a local contest. If they do well in this, regional contests may come next. After that, the next step may be to compete for their country as an amateur.

PRO SURFERS, LIKE KELLY SLATER (RIGHT), CAN MAKE A GOOD LIVING FROM PRIZE MONEY AND ENDORSEMENTS.

Turning pro

The very best amateur surfers might be lucky enough to be offered a professional ('pro') contract. This means they have achieved every surfer's dream – to be paid to go surfing! Top pro surfers travel the world, entering competitions at the best surf spots. They can earn millions of pounds from prize money and payments from surf companies.

Famous surfers

Throughout the history of surfing, some people have stood out as particular experts. These are the surfers who are thought of as the sport's greats and have earned a place in the surfing hall of fame.

Duke Kahanamoku

Olympic swimming champion in 1912 and 1920, film actor and Sheriff of Honolulu, Hawaii, Duke is said to have caught the longest wave ever. In 1932, Duke paddled out into giant waves near Diamond Head, Hawaii. The wave he caught dwarfed his 4.88-m board. Duke guessed that he rode the wave for nearly 3km.

The two Toms

Tom Curren is the son of legendary big-wave surfer Pat Curren. Tom was the first American to win the World Championship Tour title in 1985 at the age of just 19. He won two more world titles, spurred on by his rivalry with Australian Tom Carroll. Carroll also won several world championships in the 1980s. He is particularly famous for his courageous surfing at Pipeline, Hawaii's most feared surf spot.

DUKE KAHANAMOKU STANDS NEXT TO HIS ENORMOUS BOARD.

Kelly Slater

Kelly is one of the most famous surfing figures ever and earns his living from prize money and endorsing products such as clothing and computer games.

BORN	Cocoa Beach, Florida, USA, 1972
HEIGHT	1.75 m
WEIGHT	73 kg
WORLD CHAMPION	Six times (1992, 1994–98)
CAREER FACTS	Kelly was the first surfer to earn over US$1 million in prize money.

Layne Beachley

As a kid in Sydney, Australia, Layne was nicknamed 'Gidget' after the surf-mad girl in the famous movie. Today, her nickname is 'Beach', and she is the most successful female surfer ever, having won the world championships a record six times.

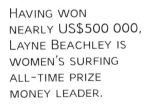

HAVING WON NEARLY US$500 000, LAYNE BEACHLEY IS WOMEN'S SURFING ALL-TIME PRIZE MONEY LEADER.

Russell Winter

Britain's number one surfer in recent years, Russell has competed on the World Championship Tour and in 2002 won the Boardmasters event in front of his home crowd.

Lisa Andersen

Born Florida, USA, Lisa ran away from home at age 16 because her parents wouldn't let her go surfing. She left a note promising that one day she would be world champion. Lisa kept her word and won five world titles from 1994 to 1998.

Surfing around the world

Most weekends there is a surf competition somewhere in the world. However, there are only a few really famous contests. Some contests are part of the World Championship Tour (WCT), while others are one-off 'speciality events'.

Teahupoo Pro, Tahiti

This WCT event is held at one of the most dangerous surf spots in the world – a reef off the coast of Tahiti. In 2004, one of the two finalists, Australian Nathan Hedge, had his arm dislocated from its socket after he wiped out in the final.

The Quicksilver In Memorial of Eddie Aikau, Hawaii

The 'Eddie' is a speciality event held at Waimea Bay, Hawaii, in memory of a famous lifeguard. It only takes place when the surf is over 6 m – which means wave faces of about 12 m.

SURF JOURNALIST
GARY TAYLOR
SAID, 'TEAHUPOO
ISN'T A WAVE,
IT'S A WAR ZONE'.

ANDY IRONS CELEBRATES WINNING THE 2003 PIPELINE MASTERS FOR THE SECOND YEAR RUNNING.

The G-land Pro, Indonesia

A WCT event held at 'G-land' (short for Gragajan) in Indonesia. Gerry Lopez, a famous Hawaiian surfer, discovered the surf spot in the 1970s. He happened to look out of the window of his plane as it was coming in to land at Jakarta and saw the perfect wave peak at G-land.

Bell's Beach Classic, Australia

This WCT event is held at Bell's Beach, Australia, around Easter. The beach is named after Martha Bell, who owned a farm that surfers had to drive through to reach the shore.

Pipeline Masters, Hawaii

This is the WCT event that most surfers want to win. Held at Pipeline on the North Shore of Oahu, Hawaii, the Masters frequently decides the world championship winner. In 2003, Andy Irons clinched the world championship beating Kelly Slater at Pipeline.

Mundaka Pro, Spain

The river mouth at Mundaka, Spain, produces huge, long rolling waves. These form the site of Europe's most important surf contest.

The J-Bay Pro, South Africa

LOCATION Cape St Francis, South Africa

DESCRIPTION A vast bay with five distinct but connected surfing areas.

HISTORY First held in 1983, the J-Bay became part of the WCT a year later.

ATTRACTIONS The competition pulls in the best surfers who are lured by the quality of the waves, as well as the prize money of US$250 000.

Surfing words

amateur Someone who is unpaid. An amateur surfer is one who does not win prize money in competitions or get paid to surf by a surf company.

bonzer A board with five fins and a deep, double-concave bottom shape.

break A wave 'breaks' when it folds over itself and rolls foaming to the shore.

concave Curving inwards. Concave-bottom boards have a bottom that curves in, rather than bulging out.

flexibility Bendiness, or being able to move your limbs easily and freely.

fibreglass A material made of fine threads of glass pressed together.

foam A light artificial material that contains air bubbles.

grommet A young surfer.

ho-dad A non-surfer or uncool person.

kahuna Hawaiian royalty or an older surfer worthy of respect.

kook A bad or inexperienced surfer.

locals The surfers who regularly surf at a particular location.

longboard A board that is 2.75 m long or more.

professional/pro Describes a surfer who gets paid to surf and tries to win prize money by entering competitions.

reef A solid underwater structure that sticks up from the sea bottom.

shaping Describes the process of creating a surfboard from a piece of wood or foam.

shortboards Boards with a narrow nose which are about 1.9 m long.

technology The use of science and machines to solve problems.

technique A skill that can be learned and used to do something.

twinnie/twin-fin A board that has two fins.

twinzer A board that has four fins, usually with one smaller fin beside each of the main ones. Twinzers are very unusual today.

vee On a vee-bottom board, the rails would be higher than the stringer if the board was laid bottom-down on the floor.

wahine Hawaiian for girl or woman.

wave face The smooth front part of a wave, before it has broken.

whitewater The white part of the wave where the water has already broken.

wipe out To fall off while surfing.

yoga A form of exercise that involves putting the body into various positions that strengthen the muscles and make the joints more flexible.

Films

Endless Summer II (1994)
Made 30 years after the original, this movie follows another group of surfers on a trip around the world.
Blue Crush (2002)
Follows a group of girl surfers as they prepare for a big competition in Hawaii.
Billabong Odyssey (2003)
A group of surfers use hi-tech weather-forecasting devices and powerful boats on a quest around the world to find and ride the biggest wave.

Books to read

To The Limit: Surfing by Paul Mason (Hodder Wayland, 2000)
Diary of a Surf Freak by Dan Johnson (Heinemann Library, 2003)
Super Sports: Water Sports by David Jefferis (Chrysalis Children's Books, 2001)

Magazines

The best British surf magazine is *Carve*. It features travel articles, board design, competition news and much more. From the USA come *Surfer* and *Surfing*. Both are similar and offer an interesting (if California-based) view of the surf world. South of the equator, *Tracks* offers the latest news for surfers in Australia, while *New Zealand Surfing Magazine* gives surfers information about the land of the long white cloud. In South Africa, *Zigzag Surfing Magazine* provides reviews of the best surfing spots around the world and its online site (www.zigzag.co.za) gives a daily surf report on South African resorts.

Index